Victimized with a Testimony

"If There Is No TEST- There Is No TESTIMONY!"

Trenton Bowens

VICTIMIZED WITH A TESTIMONY

iUniverse books may be ordered through booksellers or by contacting:

iUniverse LLC
1663 Liberty Drive
Bloomington, IN 47403
www.iuniverse.com
1-800-Authors (1-800-288-4677)

ISBN: 978-1-4502-6433-4 (sc)
ISBN: 978-1-4502-6432-7 (e)

Printed in the United States of America.

iUniverse rev. date: 09/24/2014

Dedication

This Book is dedicated to every person who is feeling trapped and wants to be free, but doesn't know how to be free. I pray God uses this book to allow you to be set free.

"It was for freedom that Christ set us free; therefore
keep standing firm and do not be subject again
to a yoke of slavery."

~ Galatians 5:1

Acknowledgements

First and foremost I would like to thank you for purchasing this book and investing in my ministry. I pray that this book is a blessing to you. I pray also that God delivers you and sets you free! After each chapter you will find Points to Ponder, in which I strongly recommend that you complete.

I believe in giving honor to people when it's due, and therefore it would be wrong for me not to give my sincere heartfelt thanks to the following people (Sorry if I missed anyone! Charge it to my head and not to my heart!!). I would like to thank my spiritual mothers, Daphne Rudley and Mother Harper. When I needed prayer, you prayed; when I needed someone to talk to, you spoke life into me. I pray God continues to bless you with wisdom and favor.

My spiritual brother, Edward Lee: Man, words can't express how I feel about you. I have never been able to tell you thanks for all the advice and for praying for me.   I pray

GOD uses you forever more and more, and continues to bless you. It's not easy being chosen!

My Godmother, Princella Tobias: Well it's almost been seven years since we met at a local church. You were my first real employer and inspired me to get into politics and writing. I would have never been able to spread my wings if you hadn't taught me how to fly. Continue to fight for what you believe in!

My very own Sis, Greta Joseph: All I had to do was ask and you said you would. I have no other words to say besides thank you! May God continue to bless you and bless Elaine's Publishing Center as your business grows!

Thanks to my Sister Natay Hollie and Greater Works 2 Prayer Support Group. Those Wednesday night prayers helped me to get back on focus in God when I went astray. Thanks for your advice and prayers; words cannot express my gratitude.

My haters: If it wasn't for you I wouldn't be where I am today. You taught me to pray more and seek God like never before. Through your work in pain, you have taught me that there is no blessing without a battle.

I decided to save the best for last!

I would like to thank my family for their ongoing support and for rooting me on when I felt like giving in and losing it. I cannot adequately express my love for you all. I love you dearly and thank God for putting you all in my life!

It would be insane and crazy if I didn't thank God for blessing me to launch this first project, and for not taking His hand off my life. Lord, even when I think I don't deserve things you continue to bless me. Lord thank you for using me to help people become free and delivered, and to walk in their calling.

Introduction
The story of Trenton M. Bowens

Imagine yourself hearing a little voice inside your head, not knowing if you're going crazy or if you're hearing the voice of God?
Imagine yourself being called a sissy, fag, or a dummy by your own family?

Imagine yourself trying to commit suicide and you can't. Every time you attempt it you don't succeed. Imagine yourself wanting to know if you are gay or straight, and you were afraid to tell anyone of your doubts?

Imagine having low self-esteem. You feel like you're worthless and never going to amount to anything, or you're going to be in jail or dead.

Well, that's what I went through all my life. I was trapped and tormented by the enemy for so long! I would visualize myself free and out of bondage, but I never knew how to cross the line to freedom.

I would often ask God, "Is this a story you want me to tell or help other individuals come out of?"   I am reminded of the scripture: *"For I know the plans I have for you," declares the LORD, "plans to prosper you and not to harm you, plans to give you hope and a future."* (Jeremiah 29:11 NIV)

Table of Contents

~Chapter One~
Generational Curses

Have you ever wondered why you go through so many different things? Was your mom an alcoholic, your sister an alcoholic, and your daddy? Did you hear people say "her daddy was like that, so she's just following his footsteps"? My brothers and sisters, that's what I call speaking generational curses, in existence,.

Did you know we have the power to speak over our children and pray curses off of them? We can speak life into our children and not death! This chapter will help you identify some of the issues from which you haven't been delivered, and see how they proceed from one generation to the next. Possibly you will see how your kids might be walking down your path.

You see, I was adopted, and didn't know my biological mother until I was 17 or 18 years old. I didn't start speaking to my biological mother until around that age. I suffered from low self- esteem and often depression. I didn't know why I often felt low, like I was the scum of the earth. When I felt depressed, I wanted to belt out and cry, but I couldn't.

Sometimes I felt like I was mourning often. It wasn't until I talked to her and she told me how she used to be depressed and down all the time. Sometimes when I used to talk to her over the phone, I would instantly get depressed. I then understood it was a generational curse. The buck stopped with me. I had to develop a strong prayer life.

Do you believe that God is Jehovah Rappha, which means "my healer"? Do you believe that the power of God can remove those generational curses? If so, say this prayer:

Father God,

I humbly ask that you remove every generational curse from my family and from my kids. Lord, I ask that you allow them to be great women of God and great men of God. I ask that you remove the spirit of homosexuality, the spirit of bitterness, the spirit of depression, the spirit of lesbianism, and the spirit of addiction. In Jesus' name Amen.

Now let me explain something to you about healing. It doesn't happen overnight. We, as Christians, sometimes believe healing is supposed to happen the next day. No, it's a process. In dealing with generational curses you have to speak to your child: "Tommy, you're going to be a great man of God. You're going to be successful and awesome."

In the Webster Dictionary, "generation" is defined as: "a body of living beings constituting a single step in the line of descent from an ancestor of individuals born and living contemporaneously."
Now the word "curse" is defined as: "a prayer or invocation for harm or injury to come upon one," or, "evil or misfortune that
Comes as if in response to imprecation or as retribution.

Do you see how generational curses cause torment in people's lives? God doesn't want us to be tormented; God wants us to be free! The enemy wants us to feel that we are trapped in a closet; he wants us to feel locked up. When you're free in God, the enemy hates it.

Praying against generational curses is tricky. You see, it's not just for that generation; you have to pray for twenty-five years before the present generation. In the book of John 14:14 it states, "You may ask me for anything in my name and I will do it."

We have to ask God to pull every demonic stronghold out of us. We have to believe that God is our Jehovah Rappha, our healer (Exodus 15:26). He can deliver us from generational curses (Galatians 5:1-13).

Brothers and sisters, so many times we doubt what God can do for us. Let me be the first to say I doubted God before, but He is surely able. We face generational curses and we don't even know it. That's not God's plan for us. God wants us to be free. Before I end this chapter I want to say a prayer for you.

Dear Lord,
We humbly ask that you remove every demonic generational curse that has been placed over us. We ask that you take them out of us. We ask that you remove them from future generations. Lord, we ask you to place the fruit of your Spirit over our lives and take any and everything that's not like you out of us. In Jesus' name we pray Amen.

We have to speak life into our children, brothers and sisters, and stop degrading them, or talking down to them, or calling them names. That can hurt a person; words do hurt! God has given us the authority to cast out demons and lay hands on the sick.

~ Points to Ponder~
I encourage you to write your answers down.
You should not limit yourself in your response.

What are some generational curses you are facing?

Do you see how generational cures can impact your
life in a positive or negative way?

What will you do to end generational Curses?

~Chapter Two~
Rejection

Have you ever realized or wondered why you don't fit in? You can say something and no one accepts it, but someone else says it and they accept it?

Nobody wants to go through rejection. It hurts, you're wondering why you never fit in the group? Or why you always seem like the weird one.

Rejection is a powerful demon that you have to overcome. It's not easy. You see, rejection is like a root; it branches off to different things. While battling generational curses, I had to fight with a few of these demonic forces: Low Self-Esteem, Homosexuality, Loneliness, Depression, and Suicide

If you're not prayed up, you could go astray. You see, I was made different. My voice was light. I wasn't the average guy, like your high school jock or the thug guy type. I was laidback; People rejected me because they thought I was different.

I often thought about the book of Jeremiah. Jeremiah was young and God called him; but he was scared because he looked different. The Lord told Jeremiah, "Before I formed you in the womb I knew you; before you were born I sanctified you; I ordained you a prophet to the nations." (Jeremiah 1:5 NIV).

I would ask myself, "Lord you knew me before you created me, is there something I need to do?" I didn't understand, but then I learned. God doesn't put anything on us that we can't bear. We have trials that become lessons learned, and we need to be able to tell others our testimony.

I was often told that "to be rejected by man is to be accepted by God". Which would you rather be? No teenager wants to be rejected; no one wants to be left out, picked on, or always considered weird.

One Pastor told me it's not easy being chosen. I didn't understand what he meant until I got older. The enemy will throw every little thing at you to try and distract you and take you out. I would leave a place and feel like they left me out, or wonder how come I wasn't good enough to do this or that.

The Webster Dictionary defines "rejection" as "the action of rejecting, or the state of being rejected." I define rejection as being rejected by man, not fitting in, and always considered the oddball. There can be so many people who don't accept you.

In order to overcome rejection you have to do the following things. Pray - make sure that you are building yourself a positive and effective prayer life. Prayer changes things

Build your relationship with God. God will bring you out of rejection. Understand that God allows things to happen in our lives for a reason. When you're feeling lost and rejected by man, get into the Word. Study the Bible. I learned that every time I was feeling lost and rejected, I would get into the Word and the LORD would take my mind off of that situation.

Before we go on to the next chapter let us pray:

Dear Heavenly Father, We come to you today asking you to remove the spirit of rejection. Lord, you said ask in your name and it shall be done. Father, we ask that you remove the spirit of rejection. Lord, we ask that you comfort them and send them the spirit of acceptance and the spirit of peace. In Jesus' name we pray, Amen.

~ Points to Ponder~
I encourage you to write your answers down.
You should not limit yourself in your response.

Describe a time when you felt rejected by a person.

Describe a time when you rejected a person.

Describe ways can rejection hurt a person?

~Chapter Three~
Low Self-esteem

Have you ever felt down and out like the scum of the earth? Have people ever made fun of you regarding your looks and the way you carried yourself? Do people always talk about you? Do people (even your family members) call you horrible names? Well, that's me. Earlier in the previous chapter I talked about rejection and I can testify and tell you that rejection branches off into several things. It's like a seed of a tree and then it grows.

Low self-esteem is a powerful demon. I suffered from low self-esteem so much that I tried to kill myself many times and was mad, when I wasn't able to do so. You would most likely be surprised that I suffered from low self-esteem.

I was very active in my younger days and received many awards and was always in the newspaper. But truthfully, I was anti-social and I didn't trust or talk to anybody.   I would walk with my head down.

People would call me names that would hurt my feelings. They would pick out every little flaw. It became a case where I didn't know who I was anymore. I didn't care about my hygiene or my appearance or anything. I began walking around with my head down and not caring.

I began to become sensitive to words. I remember chasing a kid home with scissors because I was tired of the words he was throwing at me. But then I had to accept that I wasn't your average guy. I didn't play sports. I wasn't into girls until a later age. I didn't do things that other guys did. I had a light voice and I was shy. I used to be called "ugly" and names like "fag" and other horrible things.

I was spit on and talked about. If had a pair of cross tracker shoes on, they would make fun of me. It never helped to please man. I would often be told that they talked about Jesus, too. I understood that, but I also would ask God, "Why me?" People would see my smile and think everything was okay. It wasn't. I was hurting. I was in a deep depression. I used to sneak and take medicine, thinking I would overdose, and then I couldn't.

I used to walk with my head down because I was scared to face man's persecution. I was scared of what they would say as I walked past. I had to learn and know who I was in Christ! How I may seem to you doesn't matter; it's what I am in the body of Christ that's important.

You know, low self-esteem is just not feeling ugly about yourself; you can also feel insecure; always asking people for their advice or what they think. I used to talk to young ladies that I knew had low self-esteem just to make me feel good. It was wrong of me, but it felt like I was able to relate to them and they were able to relate to me.

I wasn't into name brand clothing because my mom used to tell me, "it's not what you have on, it's the type of person you are." But after graduating from High School I decided to treat myself and purchase some expensive clothes.

   I also decided to put a texturizer kit in my hair. And I began to look different. But the truth of the matter is I still wasn't happy. I wasn't satisfied with myself; I felt like I was the scum of the earth or that ugly duckling still.

Now let me explain to you that anybody can go through low self-esteem. It doesn't just happen to a certain type of person. I had a friend who was popular in high school and was well liked, but he never had confidence in himself. He would put on shows to make people think that he had that confidence in himself, but he was struggling deep down.

We as people can cause a person to suffer from low-self-esteem by speaking ill will or negative words about a person. Life and death is in the power of the tongue! You see, the enemy likes to see you down and out, but we serve an awesome God! I am going to give you this equation: <u>Prayer + Fasting + Worship = Victory and Deliverance</u>.

You must build a prayer life. I don't know how to stress this. Without a prayer life, the enemy knows and sees that he can attack you and take you out.

The enemy wants us to sit and dwell in this little pity party. I learned that as long as I didn't know who I was or am in Christ, the enemy would taunt me and try to make me sit and dwell on that.

You have to understand that the enemy sees your anointing. His goal is to kill, steal, and destroy. You have to have that boldness and speak to that Demon! "Is that all you got, Devil?" God has given us the authority; I can't stress that enough.

People will wait for a Sunday or Bible study night, or a day in the week for the pastor to lay hands, or go to the prayer line. God has given us the authority.

The Bible tells in the Book of Corinthians. 2 Corinthians 4:8: "We are hard-pressed on every side, yet not crushed; we are perplexed, but not in despair; persecuted, but not forsaken."

Let's say a prayer. I want you to touch your stomach while praying this prayer now. Don't say this prayer if you don't want to be healed and set free!

Dear Heavenly Father,
We come before you asking you to forgive us for any sin that we have committed, knowing or unknowingly.   Lord, we ask that you remove the spirit of low self-esteem right now. Lord, you said ask and it shall be given. Lord, we demand that spirit to come out right now; we cast it out. Lord, we ask that you fill their heart with the peace and love of God. Lord, we pray and ask that you give them your DNA which is the fruit of the spirit, right now, in JESUS' name.   We cast out the spirit of low self-esteem and suicide, the spirit of cutting and harming ourselves, right now in the name of Jesus. We demand it to leave in Jesus' name, Amen,

You have to quote scriptures around your house; put them in your bathroom or in your bedroom and quote them to yourself when you need to hear the Word.

"For God so loved the world he gave his one and only son, that whoever believes in him shall not perish but have everlasting life." (John 3:16)

"I can do all things through Christ who strengthens me." (Philippians 4:13)

"You are the light of the world. A city on a hill cannot be hidden." (Matthew 5:14)

I could go on and quote scriptures that uplift my spirit and my soul, but you have to take the initiative upon yourself. Remember, God makes no mistakes in creating us. Don't let anyone tell you differently.

Did you know?

Did you know these facts about low self-esteem? According to the website Do Something.Org, listed below are some facts about low-self esteem. I can actually testify that some of these are true. I have experienced these, but thanks be to God, we understand and see how good our God is.

Low self-esteem is actually a thinking disorder in which an individual views himself as inadequate, unworthy, unlovable, and/or incompetent. Once formed, this negative view of self permeates every thought, producing faulty assumptions and ongoing self-defeating behavior.

Seven in ten girls believe they are not good enough or do not measure up in some way, including their looks, performance in school and relationships with friends and family members.

A girl's self-esteem is more strongly related to how she views her own body shape and body weight, than how much she actually weighs.

78% of girls with low self-esteem admit that it is hard to feel good in school when you do not feel good about how you look (compared to 54% of girls with high self-esteem).

75% of girls with low self-esteem reported engaging in negative activities such as disordered eating, cutting, bullying, smoking, or drinking when feeling badly about themselves (compared to 25% of girls with high self-esteem).

61% of teen girls with low self-esteem admit to talking badly about themselves (compared to 15% of girls with high self-esteem).

More than one-third (34%) of girls with low self-esteem believe that they are not a good enough daughter (compared to 9% of girls with high self-esteem).

One of the main factors in teen promiscuity is self-esteem. When a teen has little or no self-confidence, he or she will use sex as a means to build confidence.

Recent years have seen a significant increase in body dysmorphia in teen boys. This is a psychiatric disorder in which the afflicted person is excessively concerned about an imagined or minor defect in their physical features.

Teenage boys can be prone to obsessive exercising, binge eating, anorexia nervosa, bulimia, steroid abuse and diet-aid abuse.

It is estimated that about 45% of Western men are unhappy with their bodies – 25 years ago, only 15% were unhappy with their bodies.

I encourage you to write your answers down.
You should not limit yourself in your response.

Have you ever battled with low self-esteem?

Describe how you helped a person with low self-esteem?

Describe what advice would you give a person who is battling low self-esteem?

~Chapter Four~
Bitterness

The definition of bitterness means: difficult or distasteful to accept, admit, or bear: the bitter truth; bitter sorrow.

Have you ever been hurt and didn't know why? Have you asked God to help you put your faith in him, and then the results were not what you wanted?

During 2005 I lost a family member who was like my second mother. She was a woman who would tell you if you're right or wrong, and still love you.

No matter what, you could always see Christ through her. She had breast cancer, but had faith that God was going to heal her. I had faith that God was going to heal her myself; after all he is Jehovah Rappha, the God that heals.

I would watch Benny Hinn and other television evangelists, and I saw people get healed and they are still living. I remember going to church one time and I saw a person get healed from cancer.

I was upset because God took her and it was way too soon. I asked God why…but I wasn't trying to listen to him or anybody. I went into a depressed phase; I didn't want to talk to anyone besides my family.

I was upset that God did not allow me to win a local election. I had a Christian campaign slogan and used my faith in God. In fact, I felt that I was the best candidate for the job. I was active in church and was going to church on Sunday mornings, Sunday evenings, Bible study nights and midweek services.

I got hurt in the church. I couldn't let it go. I asked the question "was it really worth it?" I began going astray, and started drinking and doing things of the world.

I began questioning my faith. "Is there really a God?" "Why me Lord?" I didn't hear his voice any more. I wasn't praying; I just wanted to do me. I was mad and bitter at God. I couldn't even say a prayer. I couldn't even open my Bible. But then I had to repent and ask God to forgive me; after all I had done, who was I to be bitter at God? Who was I to have the nerve to be mad at someone who puts life

into me daily? Who gives me strength? Who
supplies me with a job?   Who makes a way out of no
way?

I felt like God left me…. but that was the enemy
working inside me.   God never leaves us. We may
leave God; but God never leaves us! I had to read
my Bible and read the story of Ruth. In the first few
chapters, it explains how Naomi lost her husband
and two sons and how she became bitter. God's
presence was invisible, but He was always there with
her.

Many times in life we can become upset and angry at
God, but we must remember that for everything
there is a season and a reason. We have to
understand that God sees fit when we don't. I had to
repent so much because I was angry, and I thought
that God wasn't allowing positions or job openings to
open up. I had to pray for a while, and ask God to
forgive me for any and everything that I had done.

If you're going through bitterness or need help, I
would like to say this prayer for you and with you.
Now I need you to touch your stomach and remove
every distraction because we're going to pray for
God to remove a demonic force that causes us to be
bitter at Him.

Dear Heavenly Father,

We humbly come before you King. We come before your face, asking you to forgive us for our sins that we have committed knowingly and unknowingly. We pray that you remove every bit of bitterness inside of our lives.

Lord, we humbly ask you to take every tormenting demon that's in our lives out of us. We cast it out right now in the name of Jesus. We ask that you remove every bit of bitterness in our heart, mind and body, right now, in the name of Jesus. Lord we ask that you forgive us for being angry at you. We ask you to forgive us for doing any and everything that is not like you. In Jesus' name we pray. Amen.

I had to understand that my aunt's healing was where she wanted to be. The Bible says to be absent from the body is to be present with the LORD. Where my aunt is right now is where I want her to be.

You see, God saw fit in this local election to allow the election to transpire as it did.   I was hurt. I only got 37 votes and the same usual suspects got in; the ones that were radical with questionable integrity. God saw fit that I didn't win.

I asked why, and did not understand why people who said they were going to help me didn't. I didn't hear a response from God. But then, a few months later, the elected officials that won the election became powerless. I wasn't ready for the position. I was battling too many issues.

We have to remember that God makes no mistakes. The enemy wants us to become angry with God and upset, and question our faith. You see, the enemy wants you to become stale in your spirit. He wants you to feel like you lost the presence of God. He wants you to question your belief in God, but I speak to the God in you. Greater is He that is in you than he that is in the world.

~ Points to Ponder~
I encourage you to write your answers down.
You should not limit yourself in your response.

Describe a time when you were upset at God and
you wanted to ask God why.

Did you see the Master's plan, or were you being
selfish?

Did you apologize or pray, and ask God to forgive
you?

~Chapter Five~
Loneliness

The definition of loneliness is an emotional state in which a person experiences a powerful feeling of emptiness and isolation.

As I got older I found out Loneliness is actually a state of mind. Loneliness causes people to feel empty, alone and unwanted. People who are lonely often crave human contact. I believe you can only overcome loneliness by prayer and fasting and building a strong relationship with GOD.

Have you ever felt ugly, and wonder when are you going to be in that perfect relationship? Have you ever asked "Why do these females or males keep denying me?"

I would often hear that I wasn't their type, or I was a "church boy". It used to be extremely funny and weird too, but I would wonder if I was going to be single for the rest of my life? I used to get jealous when I would see a young couple who seemed like they were in a perfect relationship, all cuddled up.

Earlier I told you that rejection branches off into different things. I cannot stress enough the importance of having a prayer life. You see, so far rejection has rooted into and branched off into many different things: low self-esteem, bitterness, and loneliness.

The enemy used to make me feel like there was no one for me.   I used to feel depressed and lonely. I never considered talking to cute females. As I said in the previous chapter, I suffered low self-esteem and I could only connect with a female who was going through the same thing.

I wasn't able to connect emotionally with them. I was having sex and still not happy. I would ask God, "You said you would give me the desires of my heart if I just trusted you. Lord, when is my time coming?"

The enemy would have me down thinking that no female wanted to talk to me. I didn't have any close friends because I felt like I couldn't trust anybody.

 I wanted someone to give me love. I would give people advice about relationships and tell them what to do and how to do it, and I wasn't even in a relationship myself.

I would act like I was in a relationship just to put on a show, until I had a friend tell me that I needed to stop that because I was going to make myself believe it. I felt a void in my life.

I didn't understand why my siblings could have boyfriends and girlfriends and I didn't. My friends were like sisters and brothers to me and they were older friends, in their late '30s and older than that.

I started to settle for less and started having sex and still wasn't happy. I felt like there wasn't anyone who I could confide in. I wanted a serious relationship. I saw some of my friends getting married and being in relationships. My siblings were in long-lasting relationships. I wanted to be in a relationship too.

I wanted to give that young lady my undivided attention. I wanted to be engaged at a young age and travel around. It wasn't until later in my life that the Lord explained to me that even though I was working, I was being irresponsible, spending money galore, and being irresponsible with my credit.

How could he bless me with someone in my life while I was being that irresponsible? If he sent someone to me, would my mind still be on him, or would I sway away from him?

How could I do my assignment that he had ordained me to do? How could I love someone else when I was still battling with my own self-confidence? I needed to work on loving myself and getting myself together.

Our flesh at times wants something, but God doesn't see us as ready. Remember, God makes no mistakes. Sometimes we try and rush things, and God doesn't see fit. We begin questioning God. Why is this happening to me? Why do I have to go through this? The enemy plants seeds of doubt and makes you feel lonely.

But the God in me speaks to that Demon. I, again, cannot say how important it is to have a prayer life. God answers prayers. When I strayed away from God I went to something which still gave me no happiness. The next chapter will tell you more about that.

Please always quote scriptures when you're feeling this way. Play some Gospel music, and don't allow the enemy to make you feel depressed.

"And we know that in all things God works for the good of those who love him, who have been called according to his purpose." (Romans 8:28)

"The LORD will make you the head, not the tail. If you pay attention to the commands of the LORD your God that I give you this day and carefully follow them, you will always be at the top, never at the bottom." (Deuteronomy 28:13)

"You are all sons of Light and sons of the Day. We are not of the night or darkness." (1Thessalonians 5:5)

"But those who wait on the Lord shall renew their strength; they shall mount up with wings like eagles. They shall run and not be weary; they shall walk and not faint." (Isaiah 40:31)

I know when I am feeling sad, depressed or lonely people can see that, and they don't want to be around that spirit. Nobody wants to affiliate with you. I went to a local barbershop one day and they got on me about that, and told me as best as they could.

Dear Heavenly Father,

We come to you seeking your face, and praying and asking you to take the spirit of loneliness out of us. We cast out every demonic spirit of depression, suicide and loneliness. Satan, we demand you to leave right now in the name of JESUS. Lord, we ask that you fill that void right now. In Jesus' name we pray. Amen.

Did you know Wikipedia.org lists many facts about loneliness? I believe loneliness is caused by depression and rejection, but because we serve an awesome God, we are able to be delivered and healed, and no-longer be bound.

Wikipedia says people can experience loneliness for many reasons, and many life events are associated with it. The lack of friendship relations during childhood and adolescence, or the physical absence of meaningful people around a person are causes for loneliness, depression, and involuntary celibacy. At the same time, loneliness may be a symptom of another social or psychological problem, such as chronic depression.

Many people experience loneliness for the first time when they are left alone as an infant. It is also a very common, though normally temporary, consequence of divorce or the breakup or loss of any important long-term relationship. In these cases, it may stem both from the loss of a specific person and from the withdrawal from social circles caused by the event or the associated sadness.

Loss of a significant person in one's life will typically initiate a grief response; here, one might feel lonely, even in the company of others. Loneliness may also occur after the birth of a child, after marriage or any socially disruptive event, such as moving from one's hometown to a university campus or moving into a brand new community or school. Loneliness can occur within marriages or similar close relationships where there is anger, resentment, or where the feeling of love cannot be given or received. It may represent a dysfunction of communication. Loneliness could be also caused by being in places with low population density where there are not many people for miles around to interact with you. Learning to cope with changes in life patterns is essential in overcoming loneliness.

A twin study found evidence that genetics account for approximately half of the measurable differences in loneliness among adults, which was similar to the heritability estimates found previously in children. These genes operate in a similar manner in males and females.

I encourage you to write your answers down.
You should not limit yourself in your response.

Have you ever been depressed and lonely at the same time?

What did you do to make yourself happy?

What are some words of advice you would tell a person battling loneliness?

Chapter Six
Homosexuality

If I told you my story, would you still accept me? Or would you gossip about me? If I told you my story would you look at me funny or would you still be the same? Would you rejoice with me and see how good God has been?

Well, let me give you a warning. First and foremost, this chapter is going to get raw. That's one problem with the church today. We are scared to address the raw issues.

You see, I was constantly called a "sissy" or a "fag" and other names. This can hurt a person's spirit. I used to ask myself if they thought I was gay; did they see something that I didn't see?

I knew what the Bible said; I just wasn't living by it. The Bible says God made Adam and Eve so they could become fruitful and increase in number. God didn't make Adam and Steve, or Jessica and Rachel.

Since I was six or seven I knew I had gay tendencies. I knew I was confused. I would lay up on my bed wondering if I was gay. I was scared that my family was going to disown me. I tried fighting it for far too long, and then it really happened.

Some people say they are born like that or they can't be changed. I am no scientist or Doctor. However, today's society has conducted studies to try and prove that people are born gay.

I believe a person is not born gay or a lesbian. GOD tells us to be fruitful and multiply- Adam and Steve cannot multiply nor can Jessica and Rachel.

I believe it is a small seed that the enemy plants in a person's life like rejection. It branches off in many different ways, like a tree. You see, I told you I went through the following:

- Rejection
- Low Self-esteem
- Bitterness
- Loneliness
- Homosexuality

It took me a while to understand the process of a demonic tree. When storms happen, sometimes branches can fall down and break off. So rejection was a limb, along with low self-esteem and bitterness and loneliness...but the trunk of the tree was me battling homosexuality.

I would claim deliverance and pray about it, but I was still battling it. It would come back stronger and stronger. I was of the belief that God will sometimes allow things to happen to us just to keep us running back to him.

People would call me gay, or a fag, or tell me I talked like a female and I had gay tendencies, or, "put some bass in your voice." Most of my life I was fighting that label of being called gay or fag. I didn't know if I was gay or straight.

The worst feeling is to not being able to tell your parents or siblings you may be gay or your sexual confused. The decision can hurt your family relationship or can help your family. I was scared of becoming the black sheep in my family.

People who knew me knew I was scared of being around gay people. If you said something that I considered to be gay, I would get mad. I was sensitive to that word; I didn't like you and I wanted to fight you.

I went to a local church where another young man was afflicted with that spirit, and he wanted me to try to experience it. I knew then that the enemy was working hard. I denied him, but I felt violated; I felt like I was dirty and I didn't know what to do until I told my mom.

Even at my local church one of the members, who was battling the same spirit that I was facing, laid hands on me. He was battling that spirit and was out in the open with it.

 That's when I learned that the different spirits can rest in the church. It's so important, people of God, to be prayed up and to have a prayer life; it is crucial.

 If you're not prayed up, that spirit can come upon you, and that's where it rests! Many spirits garner power from the church that's where they rest. You have your warlocks and witches and whoremongers and so many other spirits. I have personally noticed the churches are filled with the homosexuality and lesbian spirit.

Perfect Example I remember a Minister, who used to be over a department at a church was on a bisexual and gay website we both were on. We exchanged numbers he sent me a picture of himself and I was shocked and felt disgusted. I went by an aliases name I threatened to expose him to his family and church as well as his wife. But it left me confused. This man is married and has a family involved in the church, and messing around?

I had a friend who I considered to be one of my best friends. Battle homosexuality. He is out now but he kept it undercover in fact, he created a fake e-mail address, sending me e-mails, and wanting to know if I was gay.

After I discovered it was him, he then went and told everybody I was crazy and gay. The truth of the matter is he also suffered the same thing that I went through, with the name calling and low-self-esteem. He was hurt himself and he suffered low self-esteem and rejection. It seemed like he didn't have any confidence; he faced an identity crisis himself. He didn't know who to talk to or where he could get the help that he needed.

As I continue to live and see the world in a different perspective. Many people are crying out for help. But were blind to it. We allow it to go on and act like nothing is wrong.

I used to tell myself over and over that God did not make Adam and Steve, and try to force myself into talking to girls. I had a girlfriend; we talked off and on for five years. Remember, I told you earlier that I connected with people who were hurting themselves.

This young lady not only went through low self-esteem but many different battles. She had an attitude of the world being against her, when she was really against herself. She didn't have that self-confidence or that self-belief. She faced an identity battle. She wanted to be loved and didn't know how to love herself.

We would talk on the phone and talk about people who were battling the spirit of homosexuality. I knew she was battling that spirit, but didn't know how to tell her I knew about her! One time she gave me her password to her social media site and I seen a female from Chicago she was talking to. I acted like I didn't pay any attention to it. But it was confirmation of her battling it.

I didn't think she knew about me and that spirit. She was the first young lady to whom I lost my virginity. It was with mixed emotions. After having sex with her she told me she was pregnant. Soon as the words came out of her mouth I knew she was full of it.

She threatened to burn my house down and wanted an abortion. I told her she wasn't pregnant and actually thought to myself this was a get rich scheme.

I wanted her in my life, but knew I had to leave her alone. She was the type of person who thrived off drama. She loved to thrive off drama, and loved to live off the system. I had to understand and realize that she loved that spirit, and didn't really want to change.

I began talking to dudes on the down-low. I got tired of being lonely; I got really tired of it. I was getting attention from a male and no attention from females. I felt accepted by them. They could relate to me because I was hurting. I was bitter. I felt that I was useless.

I had to learn for myself that this involvement was just too much drama and confusion. I was used to dealing with people who would say that they didn't want any drama or mess, but they would be the main ones causing it. I had to ask myself who in the world wants to live with this lifestyle of the drama and stress and confusion.

I had to live my life on the verge of being scared 24/7. I would be scared that someone in my family was going to know about me or disown me. I was scared of living both lifestyles.

I was scared that every time I got sick I might have AIDS or something. I was scared of a scandal happening with me being an elected official seeing this hit the media or something.

I stopped going to Church because I was ashamed of myself. I didn't understand how people I messed with could be in the church praising God and being active in the church, or being married with a wife and kids?

How can you act like a ladies' man when deep down you're messing with men? I couldn't see how people could live their lives like there was nothing wrong.

Here I was sitting here mad at myself, washing my body because I felt like I was a scum. Wondering how could they still be active? How could they lay hands on people and pray for people when they're committing sin themselves? How can they preach to me when they're doing worse than I am?

You see, the enemy likes to play tricks and portray things as they are not. Me, I was thinking the grass was greener on the other side when it wasn't. People who are going through with this spirit like to tell people not to judge them, and try and portray it as being okay. The Devil is a liar.

The enemy knew that seed was planted already in my life. It needed some help growing, so that's why he placed those other issues that I faced into my life. And then he watered it so it could grow.

Trying to be delivered from homosexuality and wanting to be delivered are two different things. You really have to want to be delivered and not just talk about it. You see, the Bible tells us faith without works is dead. You have to show the Lord you want to be delivered.

I would go to church and get in the prayer lines, praying and asking the Lord to show it to the pastor so he could seek and cast it out of me. I was hoping they saw it in the spirit, and they would pray for me or demand it to come out of me.

I found myself in the lifestyle of trying to be delivered.   I would contact my prayer warriors and have them pray for me. But would fall right back into temptation.

I remember one time I was in the process of having sex and out of nowhere one of my prayer warriors' voices would come through my head. That voice was so loud that I had to stop what I was doing. The person then asked me, "Do you go to church?" It was one of the most awkward and most feelings.

I ended up deleting all of their numbers out of my phone. I blocked them on social media websites and tried to cut off communication with ones who were battling that spirit. Some would still call and I would be like, "Who is this?" They would get mad at me, but I was trying to better myself.

 I had one person who seriously thought it was a joke. When I did that, he only texted me for money and called me for money. Besides, he was a mess and what you call a drama king. He had a kid and used his looks and played the victim card with this horrible sad story.

Being delivered from homosexuality is a process. It takes not just one day, but it is a process. I learned that I could confess and say that I was delivered, but it was up to me to want to be delivered. Now let me make myself clear. I am not saying you cannot be delivered overnight; some people can be.

But for me it was a process. Till this day I still have to remain prayed up so I won't slip up.
I believe that God places obstacles in our lives to keep us coming back to him. I had to get deep back in my spiritual realm of God...my secret place. I had to follow the equation: **Prayer + Fasting + Worship = Victory and Deliverance.**

You see, when you're worshiping God, nothing can distract you. The Bible tells us that they that worship him must worship him in spirit and in truth. The enemy cannot distract us. You have to start fasting and praying -- build a prayer life. That's the way to communicate with God.

The Bible tells us in the book of Matthew: "And Jesus rebuked the demon, and it came out of him, and the child was cured from that very hour. Then the disciples came to Jesus privately and said, 'Why could we not cast it out?' So Jesus said to them, 'Because of your unbelief; for assuredly I say to you, if you have faith as a mustard seed, you will say to this mountain, 'Move from here to there, and it will move; and nothing will be impossible for you. However, this kind does not go out except by prayer and fasting.'" (Matthew 17:18-20)

Get into your Word. You see, the enemy's goal is to kill, steal, and destroy. The Bible tells us in the book of John: "The thief does not come except to steal, and to kill, and to destroy. I have come that they may have life, and that they may have it more abundantly." (John 10:10) We have to pray and ask God to decrease flesh and increase us with his spirit.

If you're not prayed up then flesh can overtake you. Going to church every Sunday is not going to deliver you. We have to put some type of action with our faith.

Sexual perversion is a powerful demon. Sex is designed for men and women when they are married; it's a great thing. Nowadays sex is so overrated; it's just about in every movie. In today's society the music you listen to talks about sex. Kids don't even know what sex is all about. But they are talking about sex. When I first had sex with a female I was like what's all the hype? Sex when you're married is one of the most beautiful things.

Our society has failed this generation with the knowledge of safe sex and what sex is meant to be for. I believe that's why we have so many single parents and so many sexual transmitted diseases running around.

We have married men putting on a façade and acting like everything is perfect, but cheating on their wives and so on. Sexual prevision is a powerful spirit

We as believers and humans also have to be careful of what we watch and listen to. All music is not good music; it's the message in the music that's important. We can watch a movie and see a sex scene, and could be masturbating while we're watching it. You could be listening to a music video or song, and then began thinking about sex afterwards.

Brothers and sisters, God is a forgiving God. Please don't let anyone tell you differently. For far too long I allowed the enemy to hold my past before me. I now refuse to care what people think about me or what they say about me. You may be considered something rude and ruthless in somebody else is eye. But In GOD's eye you're a giant in the kingdom.

We have to remember that if it wasn't for his Glory, there would be no story. For far too long I walked with my head down, scared of what people thought, and I would be scared of the chatter and the faces of people. But I know who I am in Christ and I know my father makes no mistakes; he is a forgiving God. And that's what makes all the difference.

"Therefore there is now no condemnation for those who are in Christ Jesus, because through Christ Jesus the law of the spirit of life set me free from the law of sin and death." (Romans 8:1) Don't let something that's temporary in your life become a permanent thing. Homosexuality is a powerful demonic force. You may not even be battling homosexuality; it could be lesbianism, or being addicted to porn, or constantly masturbating, or having a perverted mind, but none of these need to be permanent.

Do you really believe that you can be healed, set free, and delivered? You have to have faith. If you don't have faith, then you don't believe God can heal you. The Bible tells us in the book of Hebrews: "Now faith is being sure of what we hope for and certain of what we do not see." (Hebrews 11:1) Understand that faith is dead without works; you must exercise your faith.

We as Christians need to stop acting like this issue isn't in the church, especially the African-American church. We see them grow up in the church and are scared to say anything, but we will be the first to talk about them behind their backs, instead of praying and speaking life into the young men and women who are struggling to find their way.

Even most recently with the President coming out in favor for same sex marriage. The Church was going crazy and upset but in reality the President did not take oath to hold to uphold the bible.

He took oath to up hold the constitution that all men are created equal. We have gotten those 2 things mixed up. Morally we may believe it's wrong. But the president is not the president of religion nor is he obligated to uphold the Christian values or beliefs.

I have seen families destroyed by the way they treat their kids and siblings; treating them like they are outcasts. They don't know how to show the love of God. Parents can and will talk about people battling that spirit, saying hurtful things, and that blocks a person out. It's not going to bring them back in.

The church today has become something it's not. People are scared to cry out for help because they are tired of the gossip and the spectators. You know how, after service, the cliques talk. The church is a place for sick people seeking healing and deliverance. The church has cut the praise and worship services short; some have even cut the testimony out. Back in the day, testimony service used to help you and inspire you, and make you feel that you could make it.

I used to be scared to tell my testimony because I was scared of what the spectators would say. But remember, when God brings you out, don't be ashamed of your testimony. If a person talks about your testimony, God still gets the glory.

Before we go into prayer we need to say this affirmation. I believe that any declaration outside of the will of God is witchcraft. Now I encourage you to copy, cut and paste this, and post this wherever you can, and say this daily:

I declare God; the battle is already won. God is removing the enemy.

I declare that my God will take care of the enemy that has come against me and what God has ordained for me.

I declare that God has healed me from every sick and demonic demon.

I will live and not die, but declare the works of the Lord. Amen!

Let me also explain that I believe God will place situations in our lives to keep us saved and to always keep us in that prayer life style. Sometimes our flesh wants something and we have to go into our secret place and pray, "Lord, deliver me from my wants and give me my needs."

Remember, deliverance is a process and it's not an overnight thing. I personally still struggle with this process. We will need to go into prayer asking God to deliver and bind the spirit of perversions, the spirit of homosexuality, and the spirit of lesbianism. Now you have to have faith that God is going to deliver you, because faith without works is dead. You have to exercise your faith. Follow the equation: <u>Prayer + Fasting + Worship = Victory and Deliverance.</u>

Dear Heavenly Father,

We come before you seeking your face and seeking your deliverance. Father God, you said ask and it shall be given. Lord, deliver us from the demonic force of homosexuality. We bind you right now in the name of Jesus Christ, and declare that all of your works, roots, and spirits be cast out right now. In the name of Jesus, we command it to come out. Lord, we cast out the spirit of pedophilia. We cast out the spirit of curiosity, right now, in the name of Jesus. Lord, we ask that you make us more like you. Lord, we pray that you mold us more like you. In Jesus' name, Amen.

I encourage you to write your answers down.
You should not limit yourself in your response.

Describe do you think people are born as
homosexuals or lesbians?

Have you ever talked about or made fun of a person
battling that spirit?

Do you look differently at people who consider
themselves gay or lesbians?

~Chapter Seven~
Church Hurt

Have you ever been excited and eager to worship God? You get involved and commit your time...and then get hurt by a few?

Part of my story started off in the church. Say what you want, I was attending church Sunday morning and evening, Wednesday night Bible study, and Thursday night worship. I felt a passion. I was on fire for GOD. It felt like I was able to relate and understand the Word... I was able to study and to minister to people. I had often heard the phrase, "Church hurt is the worst hurt," but never thought about it until it affected me. It can either make you or break you.

You know how some churches have those cliques and picks? Some don't even have picks, but just bench pastors and individual leaders who try to run things, and try to out- sing the choir director and stuff. You see, for far too long I used to allow people to hurt me in the church and not say anything. I would come home and explain my anger to my sister and siblings. I was just too laidback.

Well, I used to go to a local church in Michigan. I just wanted to build God's Kingdom, see souls won, and people set free. But, as in every church, you have those few people who think that they are the pastors and try to run things.

I remember one time the Youth Group at our Church was having a function, and some inappropriate language was being spoken. As a youth leader, I went and discussed this matter with the head of the Youth Ministry. Another youth minister got upset that I hadn't told him instead. Well, in anger and in flesh, he openly screamed at me. This was not only embarrassing, but it hurt my spirit. I couldn't forgive him, and I couldn't stand to hear his voice over the pulpit. And not only that, I couldn't see how he was getting praise and worship on and I am hurt. I was angered and wanted to expose him myself.

Another example of me getting hurt in the church was by an older member. I was in charge of a fundraiser doing discount cards for the youth department. It was probably naïve and irresponsible for me to have taken the leadership of that. What was I thinking? Not only was I cheated out and played, but even adults in the church got over on me. One lady in fact called me a liar and tried to make it seem like I didn't know what I was talking about, and I had her name written down. But the hurt came from how rudely she was speaking to me, and how bold she was to call me a liar. She had not only caused me to question her integrity, but also caused problems in other young people's lives.

It took me dishing out $700 personally to end the matter. I requested and asked repeatedly and begged the church for help, but no help came my way. It was spoken, but never done. Bill collectors kept calling me, harassing me, scaring me.
I was only 17, so I didn't know what to do. I was scared my credit was going to get messed up.

Then one man over the media ministries accused me of stealing money, which was childish because I was working and making my own money. In fact, I had just been awarded a grant of $15,000 -- who needed those few dollars? And then for him to confront me at a funeral -- that was even more sickening to me. I lost all respect for him as a person. People think they can talk to any person or accuse any person.

I had all these grudges against these people. I didn't understand how they could worship and praise God;

how they could get up to sing in the choir or preach or be the worship leader. I am like, "Really, you just did this to me?" I even stopped going to church because my spirit was hurt. But then the Bible tells us in the book of Matthew: "But I say unto you, that for every idle word men may speak they will give account of it in the Day of Judgment." (Matthew 12: 36)

You know, I ended up praying and reading that scripture over and over. It's powerful because it says, "for every word you spoke or said to a person, you will have to give account." The Bible also says: "Touch not my anointed one, and do my prophet no harm." So, for everything we do, we have to give account.

We have to remember that everybody is not prayed up. We suffer a battle with flesh and with spirit. Sometimes, if you're not prayed up, flesh will overtake you and cause you to do things that you shouldn't. This may seem petty to you for me to call this church hurt, but trust me, it's the simple things that can hurt a person. The enemy used this church hurt to allow me to back slide and dwell in the past. Here they were, worshiping God and praising God, and I am sitting here hurt.

The enemy wanted me to stay in that mind frame, but holding onto grudges only hurts more. I began to feel awkward being around them and I wanted to find a way to pay them back, but this scripture would always come to my mind: "Repay no one evil for evil. Have regard for good things in the sight of all men. If it is possible, as much as it depends on you, live peaceably with all men. Beloved do not avenge yourself, but rather, give no place to wrath; for it is written, 'Vengeance is mine, I will repay,' Says the Lord'. (Romans 12:17-19) It wasn't until later that the Lord delivered me from the hurt and pain. The Lord spoke to me, telling me to LET GO.

I had to take heed to that, and cast the dead weight down. It's like in the Book of Acts when Paul was bitten by that poisonous snake and he just shook it off. Now, this snake was a deadly snake; it could have killed him instantly.

If you don't believe me, read what the Bible says: "But when Paul had gathered a bundle of sticks and laid them on the fire, a viper came out because of heat, and fastened on his hand. So when the natives saw the creature hanging from his hand, they said to one another, 'no doubt this is a murderer, whom though he has escaped the sea, yet justice does not allow him to live.' But he shook off the creature into the fire and suffered no harm.

However, they were expecting that he would swell up or suddenly fall down dead. But after they had looked for a long time and saw no harm come to him, they changed their minds and said that he was God." (Acts 28: 3-6)

Sometimes you have to shake things off: don't sweat the small stuff. The enemy's goal is to kill, steal and destroy. He wants to take you out. He will do any and every little thing to take you out. Personally, I was battling all of these battles while mentally unstable and hurt.

Remember, brothers and sisters, we are all flesh and we are prone to make mistakes. We must pray daily that God takes the flesh out of us and increases us with his spirit. Now brothers and sisters, when you feel a person has hurt your spirit or offended you, let them know. The Bible tells us in the book of Ephesians: "Be angry and do not sin: do not let the sun go down on your wrath." (Ephesians 4:26)

I have to tell you again -- don't be silent. For far too long I wouldn't speak out when I felt like I was being mistreated or used. Don't stop fellowshipping with the people of God. That's what the enemy wants you to do.

Surround yourself with some prayerful women and men of God. Don't stop going to church or Bible Studies. You see, we all are flesh, and we all can make mistakes.

Don't have the mind frame that church people don't make mistakes. They can make mistakes too, and some of the biggest mistakes at that.

Brothers and sisters let us go into prayer,

Dear Heavenly Father,
We come to you asking you to remove any grudge or hurt that's in our hearts right now. In the name of Jesus, Lord, e ask that you loose every and any demonic force that's inside of us. Lord, we ask that you remove the burden of hurt, and place the spirit of forgiveness in our heart! Lord, you said if we ask in your name it shall be done. Lord, we are asking for deliverance from church hurt right now, in Jesus' name. Amen.

Place yourself in the Word and not on people

I encourage you to write your answers down.
You should not limit yourself in your response.

Describe a point in time when you were hurt in the church.

Why did you feel more hurt in the church than when someone hurt you in the world?

Describe a time you tried to help a person who went astray because of church hurt?

~Chapter Eight~
Torment

Have you ever wanted to leave your past behind you and not worry about what people thought? Have you ever wanted to give people advice, but you were afraid of your past?   Have you ever cried or beat yourself up while holding onto your past?

For far too long I wanted to be delivered...and didn't know how. I wanted to be all that I could be in Christ. I wanted to witness to souls and see people saved, delivered, and healed. I wanted to leave my past behind me.   I wanted to look beyond my past...but somehow, someway, the enemy was taunting and teasing me. I wanted and tried to kill myself so many times, but I was unsuccessful.

Now the definition of tormenting is: "To cause to undergo great physical pain or mental anguish. To annoy, pester or harass."   For far too long I used to allow the enemy to harass me with my past hurt.   I would be speaking that I was healed, but then having second thoughts.   Brothers and sisters, that's dangerous. You have to have faith. Never, I mean NEVER, doubt your faith.

Brothers and sisters understand that God has brought you out of your past and delivered you into your present. Never doubt what God can do.   I can't lie to you -- I doubted God before, but I knew it.   I started questioning my faith. You see, the enemy wants to see you tormented and feeling bad.

I used to want to run away from my past.   I tried to act like it never happened and I was a little old angel. But truthfully it was like I was locked up and crying for freedom. I didn't know what to do or where to go to seek help. I would cry and ask God to take the torment out of me, but the enemy would always bring up my past.

I learned that in order to come out of this situation, I had to face it head on. You see, I had to expose what I was going through and speak out about it to my brothers and sisters in Christ. I had to understand that the enemy is seeking to devour whomever he may devour. The Bible tells us: "Be sober. Be vigilant; because your adversary the devil walks about like a roaring lion, seeking whom he may devour. Resist him steadfast in the faith, knowing that the same sufferings are experienced by your brotherhood in the world." (I Peter 5:8-9)

I refuse to be bound anymore. Yes, I battled homosexuality. Yes, I tried to kill myself. Yes, I thought I was the scum of the earth...but that was my past. Now, I am more than a conqueror! As it says in Romans 8:37: "Yet in all these things we are more than conquerors through Him who loved us."

For so long I had thought myself to be free, but I didn't know how to grasp and begin walking into the freedom. I didn't understand why I was scared to tell my testimony. The enemy would invoke fear into me.

God has not ordained for us to be tormented; he has ordained and created us to be free. "The thief does not come except to steal, and to kill, and to destroy. I have come that they may have life, and that they may have it more abundantly." (John 10:10)

Now, when you define the word "abundantly" the definition is "plentiful: present in great quantities, or well-supplied: providing a more than plentiful supply of something abundant in natural resources."

When you look at the definition of "Freedom," we get this definition: "the ability to act freely; a state in which somebody is able to act and live as he or she chooses, without being subject to any undue restraints or restrictions; or, released from captivity or slavery; released from being physically bound or from being confined, enslaved, captured or imprisoned."

Brothers and sisters, after reading that, you should have been shouting for joy! God has given us life so that we may live it more abundantly. God has given us freedom; he has set us free. There are no longer any chains holding us down. You have to speak victory over yourself and pray and wage warfare for God.

The Bible tells us in the book of John 8:36: "Therefore if the son makes you free, you shall be free indeed." In the book of Galatians 5:1, it tells us to "Stand fast therefore in the liberty by which Christ has made us free, and do not be entangled again with a yoke of bondage." Brothers and sisters, when the enemy starts playing with your mind, making you feel like your past is unforgiving, and you're unable to move on, pray this prayer.

Dear Heavenly Father,
We come to you today seeking your face and asking you to remove every demonic force out of us that's not of you. Lord, we ask that you remove the tormenting demon; take it out of us right now in the name of JESUS. Lord, you said if we ask in your name it shall be done. Lord, we know all things work for the good of them that love you. Lord, we pray and seek your deliverance from the tormenting demon right now. In Jesus' name, Amen.

Remember, God has ordained us to be free!

~ Points to Ponder~
I encourage you to write your answers down.
You should not limit yourself in your response.

Describe a point in time when you were afraid of
your past?

Describe how you built yourself up stronger and not
let your past get to you?

What advice would you tell someone who is battling
being tormented?

~Chapter Nine~
Deliverance

In today's society we get so caught up in going to church and going to the prayer lines when we need prayer and deliverance from an issue or a battle we are going through. Some people think that deliverance is supposed to happen instantly when being prayed for or hands being laid on.

Now I am not saying receiving prayer is a bad thing. What gets me is people think it is okay to go up to the prayer line for the same thing every Sunday, and not surround themselves with godly people. They're only getting into the word of God on Sundays, and they are not fasting; that's what I have a problem with.

When you define the word deliverance, it means rescue from something: rescue from captivity, hardship, and domination by evil. Now we know already that the Bible tells us in

Matthew 17:18-20: "And Jesus rebuked the demon, and it came out of him, and the child was cured from that very hour. Then the disciples came to Jesus privately and said, 'Why could we not cast it out?' So Jesus said to them, 'Because of your unbelief; for assuredly I say to you, if you have faith as a mustard seed, you will say to this mountain, 'Move from here to there, and it will move; and nothing will be impossible for you. However, this kind does not go out except by prayer and fasting.'"

We know that we must follow the equation **Prayer + Fasting + Worship = Victory and Deliverance.** Now you have to have faith that God is going to deliver you, because faith without works is dead; so you have to exercise your faith.

In order to experience your deliverance you have to have the spirit of expectation. Look in the Bible; in the book of Matthew 8:2-3 it talks about the man with leprosy. "And behold a leper came and worshiped him and said, 'Lord, if you are willing you can make me clean.' Jesus put out his hand and touched him, saying 'I am willing. Be clean.' Immediately his leprosy was cleansed."

The story of the man with leprosy shows that he had faith and trusted in God and he was expecting a healing.

So now we know that deliverance can't happen without faith and expectation. I can testify that when I was battling low self-esteem I wanted to come out of that phase in my life, but I wasn't expecting and seeking God to deliver me. The Bible tells us in Proverbs 3:5-6: "Trust in the Lord with all your heart and lean not on your own understanding; in all your ways acknowledge Him, and He shall direct your path." This scripture is crucial and powerful; we have to trust in God and have faith when seeking deliverance.

When I decided to run for public office a few years ago I used the slogan, "Just have faith." It was powerful to me and will remain my theme still, if I ever decide to pursue that route again.

In the book of Hebrews it tells us, "Now faith is being sure of what we hope for and certain of what we do not see." (Hebrews 11:1). The spectators may not see you being delivered out of your situation or whatever you're going through, but you have to keep that scripture foremost in your mind at all times! We are sure of what we hope for and certain of what we do not see.

You can never lose sight of your faith. In Matthew 14:28-31 it states: "And Peter answered him, Lord, 'if it is you, command me to come to you on the water.' So he said, 'Come,' and when Peter had come down out of the boat, he walked on the water to go to

Jesus. But when he saw that the wind was boisterous, he was afraid; and began to sink. He cried out, saying 'Lord, save me!' And immediately Jesus stretched out his hand and caught him, and said to him, 'O you of little faith, why did you doubt?'"

As you can see, Peter was walking on the water and began to sink when he started to doubt.   Don't doubt your deliverance from whatever you're going through; don't lose your focus or faith! Brothers and sisters, if you're not following the equation above in the earlier chapter of <u>Prayer + Fasting + Worship = Victory and Deliverance</u>, then you're not going to get delivered. You have to show some works.   Faith without works is dead!

Dear Heavenly Father,
We come before you asking in your name and seeking your deliverance from every demonic stronghold that's in our lives. Lord, we ask that you remove the spirit of doubt, the spirit of fear. Satan, we command you to flee right now in the name of JESUS. Lord, you said anything we ask for shall be done, and we are asking right now, Lord. Remove them out of us and deliver us, in your Holy Name we pray. Amen.

I encourage you to write your answers down.
You should not limit yourself in your response.

Ask yourself what are you seeking deliverance from?

Have you ever lost faith in the process of seeking
your deliverance?

Describe what advice would you tell someone who is
seeking deliverance?

~Chapter Ten~
Walking in your Calling

Have you ever felt that your purpose in life was never defined? You didn't know what to do or where you were going? You may have been working at a job and been unsuccessful, or you were making money but not happy?

You don't know where your passion lies? Or what your next move is going to be? Or what's going to happen if you were to lose your job? When is the last time you asked or listened to the voice of God? Or asked God to show you your purpose?

For far too long I wasn't happy with myself. So many people would tell me that I was called to minister; that I was a pastor, and God was going to use me to help bring in souls. I was going to be a successful man.

I created my very own non-profit organization at the age of 16 that accumulated $46,000. I got to travel around and meet well-respected people in high authority.   But I still didn't understand my calling.

It wasn't until a few years later that I decided to start writing in a local newspaper. I was writing what was on my mind and what the Lord was giving me. I wrote about my experiences and what the Lord was giving me.

Brothers and sisters, I believe we have a calling in life, and we are each called to do something important. Many times we tend not to want to hear the voice of God. A great lesson about the voice of God is in the Book of 1st Samuel; he was hearing a voice, and kept thinking it was Eli calling when it was really the Lord who was calling him. We're just too busy to listen, and sometimes think it's our mind playing tricks on us, but God could be trying to send us somewhere.

In this final chapter I am going to make it quick and to the point, so you have to understand.

Prayerfully, you have to start building your prayer life. I would recommend getting a prayer warrior, for the Bible tells us when two or three touch and agree, then Jesus is there with them.

"Assuredly, I say to you, whatever you bind on earth will be bound in heaven, and whatever you loose on earth, will be loosed in heaven. Again, I say to you that if two of you agree on earth concerning anything they ask, it will be done for them by my

Father in heaven. For where two or three are gathered together in my name, I am there in the midst of them." (Matthew 18:18-20)

Don't become a S.O.M. (Sunday Only Member). In order to find out what your gift is, you have to abstain from being an S.O.M. member. That's just leaving you open for the enemy.

Get involved with the ministry. When I was a baby saint I started working with the Children's ministry, then the Sound ministry, and then the Young Teen ministry. I then found out that my ministry was empowering believers about the goodness of the Lord through writing and telling them my TESTIMONY.

We each have a gift and a calling, brothers and sisters. Don't let that calling get wasted. Pray and ask God to show you your Gift. Until your purpose lines up with God's purpose, you will never be happy or fulfilled. Everything that you want to be successful at and secured in just won't happen unless you're lined up with God...

~ Points to Ponder~
I encourage you to write your answers down.
You should not limit yourself, in your response.

Have you prayed and asked God what your calling is?

What do you think your calling is?

Describe what are you doing to walk in your calling?

~Afterword~

Thanks for purchasing this book and reading it! Some may not understand the aim of this book. I pray it gives you a deeper connection with God and the power of prayer. In this world that we live in, we face a constant battle with sin. There is sin right there in the church as we speak.

My battle with rejection, generational curses and homosexuality was and still is a constant battle, but nothing is impossible with GOD. We must remain steadfast and remember to pray and fast.

Autobiography

Trenton Bowens was born in Columbia, Missouri on August 12, 1988 to Kathy Brookins and Fredrick Thompson. He was later adopted by David and Deborah Bowens. Trenton has four brothers and sisters, and has lived in New York, Iowa, Missouri, and Michigan.

Trenton graduated from Benton Harbor High School in 2007 and later enrolled at the University of Phoenix. Trenton was blessed and fortunate to serve on many community service boards and organizations.

He was the Founder and Director of Benton Harbor Youth-in-Government, which was the first and only organization oriented for and operated by youth in Benton Harbor, Michigan.   Under his leadership the organization, which started with a budget of zero, raised over $45,000. The organization was also the first to host debates, Youth Elections and many other events. The program was later named Project Cool by the Neighborhood Association of Michigan. Trenton helped shape the role of young people in the city of Benton Harbor, making it clear that there is no limit to what youth can do.

Trenton received the Martin Luther King Youth Humanitarian Award in 2005 for his hard work and determination while working with the city of Benton Harbor.

In 2006 Trenton lobbied on behalf of Benton Harbor Youth-In-Government to the City of Benton Harbor for vacant property which was located across the street from the Benton Harbor High School. This property was used to create a youth community garden.

During 2007 Trenton was nominated by the City of Benton Harbor for his volunteer services and his willingness and determination to make the City of Benton Harbor a better place. Trenton received the Volunteer of The Year Award.

During the spring of 2009 Trenton launched his campaign for Commissioner-at-large for the City of Benton Harbor. Trenton brought awareness to the issues that affected the working class and everyday citizen.

He also inspired many young people, letting them know that there is "No Limit," and to "Just Have Faith". During 2011 Trenton Bowens decided to run for City Commissioner again. He won with over 85 percent of the vote.

BIBLE SCRIPTURES

Throughout this book you were able to read scriptures from the Holy Bible. These particular scriptures have helped me when I was at my worst point, and I thought it would be vital to include them here. These scriptures come from the New International Version and the New King James Version.

"For I know the plans I have for you, declares the Lord, Plans to give you hope and a future." (Jeremiah 29:11, New International Version)

"You may ask me for anything in my name and I will do it."   (John 14:14)

"The righteous will live by his faith." (Habakkuk 2:4)

"You are the light of the world. A city on a hill cannot be hidden." (Matthew 5:14)

"And we know that in all things God works for the good of those who love him, who have been called according to his purpose." (Romans 8:28)

"Therefore there is now no condemnation for those who are in Christ Jesus, because through Christ Jesus the law of the spirit of life set me free from the law of sin and death." (Romans 8:1)
"Now faith is being sure of what we hope for and certain of what we do not see." (Hebrews 11:1)

"The LORD will make you the head, not the tail. If you pay attention to the commands of the LORD your God that I give you this day and carefully follow them, you will always be at the top, never at the bottom." (Deuteronomy 28:13)

"Before I formed you in the womb I knew you: Before you were born I sanctified you; I ordained you a prophet to the nations." (Jeremiah 1:5, New King James Version)

"For God so loved the world he gave his one and only son, that whoever believes in him shall not perish but have everlasting life." (John 3:16)

"I can do all things through Christ who strengthens me." (Philippians 4:13)

"You are all sons of Light and sons of the Day. We are not of the night or darkness." (1Thessalonians 5:5)

"But those who wait on the Lord shall renew their strength; they shall mount up with wings like eagles.

They shall run and not be weary; they shall walk and not faint." (Isaiah 40:31)

"And Jesus rebuked the demon, and it came out of him, and the child was cured from that very hour. Then the disciples came to Jesus privately and said, 'Why could we not cast it out?' So Jesus said to them, 'Because of your unbelief; for assuredly I say to you, if you have faith as a mustard seed, you will say to this mountain, 'Move from here to there, and it will move; and nothing will be impossible for you. However, this kind does not go out except by prayer and fasting.'" (Matthew 17:18-20)

"But I say unto you, that for every idle word men may speak they will give account of it in the Day of Judgment." (Matthew 12: 36)

"Repay no one evil for evil. Have regard for good things in the sight of all men. If it is possible, as much as it depends on you, live peaceably with all men. Beloved do not avenge yourself, but rather, give no place to wrath; for it is written, 'Vengeance is mine, I will repay,' Says the Lord'. (Romans 12:17-19)

"But when Paul had gathered a bundle of sticks and laid them on the fire, a viper came out because of heat, and fastened on his hand. So when the natives saw the creature hanging from his hand, they said to one another, 'no doubt this is a murderer, whom though he has escaped the sea, yet justice does not allow him to live.' But he shook off the creature into the fire and suffered no harm. However, they were expecting that he would swell up or suddenly fall down dead. But after they had looked for a long time and saw no harm come to him, they changed their minds and said that he was God." (Acts 28: 3-6)

"Be angry and do not sin: do not let the sun go down on your wrath." (Ephesians 4:26)

"Be sober. Be vigilant; because your adversary the devil walks about like a roaring lion, seeking whom he may devour. Resist him steadfast in the faith, knowing that the same sufferings are experienced by your brotherhood in the world." (I Peter 5:8-9)

"Yet in all these things we are more than conquerors through Him who loved us."   (Romans 8:37)

"The thief does not come except to steal, and to kill, and to destroy. I have come that they may have life, and that they may have it more abundantly." (John 10:10)

"Therefore if the son makes you free, you shall be free indeed." (John 8:36)

"Stand fast therefore in the liberty by which Christ has made us free, and do not be entangled again with a yoke of bondage." (Galatians 5:1)

"And behold a leper came and worshiped him and said, 'Lord, if you are willing you can make me clean.' Jesus put out his hand and touched him, saying 'I am willing. Be clean.' Immediately his leprosy was cleansed." (Matthew 8:2-3)

"Trust in the Lord with all your heart and lean not on your own understanding; in all your ways acknowledge Him, and He shall direct your path." (Proverbs 3:5-6)

"And Peter answered him, Lord, 'if it is you, command me to come to you on the water.' So he said, 'Come,' and when Peter had come down out of the boat, he walked on the water to go to Jesus. But when he saw that the wind was boisterous, he was afraid; and began to sink. He cried out, saying 'Lord, save me!' And immediately Jesus stretched out his hand and caught him, and said to him, 'O you of little faith, why did you doubt?'" (Matthew 14:28-31)

"Assuredly, I say to you, whatever you bind on earth will be bound in heaven, and whatever you loose on earth, will be loosed in heaven. Again, I say to you that if two of you agree on earth concerning anything they ask, it will be done for them by my Father in heaven. For where two or three are gathered together in my name, I am there in the midst of them." (Matthew 18:18-20)

Definitions

Throughout this book you will have seen some of these words. I felt led to identify each word with their definition.

Homosexuality: Sexual orientation to persons of the same sex.

Depression: The condition of feeling sad or despondent.

Bitterness: Distasteful or distressing to the mind; *a bitter sense of shame.*

Church: A body or organization of religious believers.

Hurt: A feeling of physical pain or discomfort; mental distress or anguish.

Self-esteem: Pride in oneself; self-respect.

Generation: A body of living beings constituting a single step in the line of descent from an ancestor.

Curses: An appeal or prayer for evil or misfortune to befall someone or something.

Loneliness: Without companions; alone; a feeling of bleakness or desolation.

Rejection: The act of rejecting or the state of being rejected.

Torment: To cause to undergo great physical pain or mental anguish.

Deliverance: Rescue from bondage or danger.

Prayer: A reverent petition made to God, a god, or another object of worship.

Fasting: To eat very little or abstain from certain foods, especially as a religious discipline.

Worship: Reverence offered a divine being; an act of expressing such reverence.

Faith: Firm belief in something for which there is no proof; complete trust.

~Bibliography~

Scriptures were taken from The Holy Bible, New International Version®, Copyright© 1973, 1978, 1984 Biblical. Used by permission of Zondervan. All rights reserved.

Scriptures were also taken from The Holy Bible, New King James Version, which is printed and produced by Thomas Nelson Inc.

Definitions were used from the Webster Dictionary Online, using the website of
www.merriam-webster.com

Do something.Org was used for research on low self-esteem.

Front and back covers were designed by Triple Seven Graphix, located in Benton Harbor, Michigan.

Editing was done by Elaine's Publishing Center of Benton Harbor, Michigan.

Special thanks are given to the Benton Spirit Community Newspaper, www.bentonspirit.com

Booking

Do you have an event coming up?
Do you have an event at which you
would like Trenton to speak?
Email our booking team at:
Trenton.Bowens@yahoo.com
Our staff would be more than
happy to review your request.

Website

Be sure to check out my website at
www.TrentonBowens.com
You will be able to review our upcoming events and review our blogs and upcoming web show.